WHY SOME SUCCEED
AND
OTHERS FAIL

The reason many people remain poor is because they pay more attention to limitation than abundance.

Luther Strong

www.trafford.com
North America & international
toll-free: 1 888 232 4444 (USA & Canada)
phone: 250 383 6864 ♦ fax: 812 355 4082

PREFACE

WHY SOME SUCCEED AND OTHERS FAIL

is one of the most amazing and informative books you will ever study. This book was created to help you reach your goals in life through proper thinking. My goal as a writer is to make available a book that will provide tools with which you can examine and adjust your thinking so you can learn the steps that lead to a happy, rich, and successful life in health, wealth and business.

I want our children also, to be skilled in understanding and using their mind power early in life.

I grew up where being in want was just a way of life. Poverty ruled our life. My mother did all she knew to give us the basic necessities of life. And I love her for that. It was not easy raising five children alone. It was only after many years of making mistakes, and failed relationships that I began to understand the power within me.

The only way to get away from the negative suggestion of poverty in your life is to make a complete "about face". Fear is the greatest inhibitor of all. More dreams and aspirations have been distorted because of a lie that we believed about our self and our abilities.

We were never trained to truly understand the power of the human Will in terms of gaining access to its' full potential. This power of your mind must be awakened and developed by active USE.

We must learn to let our subconscious do most of the work. That is its' business. Most of your creative mind-power is in your subconscious mind.

As a man thinks so he is, as a man thinks so shall he become.

No matter what road we take, our ultimate goal is happiness! Happiness is something different to every person in the world! Happiness is a state of mind, and the most important aspect of happiness is our pursuit of perfection in everything we attempt in life!

True success incorporates the following elements: God, Self, Family, Business, and Community.

You are a great creation; one of the finest and most precious beings in existence today. Man hasn't begun to understand all of the complexities he is made of. When we take the time to think about the universe of our mind and body, we will realize we are one of the most remarkable phenomena in existence.

No limit is placed upon man except the limits man places on himself.

THE AUTHOR

Luther Strong is a Vietnam Veteran (RANGER) United States Army. He attended National College of Business majoring in Business Administration and Marketing.

He managed several retail department stores prior to owning and operating a successful commercial landscaping and sprinkler business. He founded and presided over THE CREATIVE CENTER; a center for the artistic development of young people. Luther has over 20 years experience as an ordained minister and has been a full time pastor.

Luther's experience has given him insight into the keys that unlock the secret to a better life. After retiring in 1995, his mission is to help others learn, understand, and utilize the principles that lead to happiness and the attainment of their goals in life.

DEDICATION

This book is dedicated to my three sons, Jason B. Strong, Nicholas W. Strong, and Nigel W. Strong.

They have truly been my inspiration for this book. Every parent's dream is to have their children reach their own goals in life and be happy. With the proper training and support they will recognize their success early in life.

Thanks to my wife Marguerite Strong for her editing skills and valuable insight into this book. Thanks also to my sister Alda Jones for her continued support and encouragement throughout this project. Special acknowledgement to Byron Armstead for being a special part of our family and an encouragement to my younger sons.

TABLE OF CONTENTS

HONESTY AND SINCERITY

We have two things that we can give in this world; one is honesty and the other is sincerity! For true honesty and sincerity, we must start with ourselves. Be honest with yourself! Be sincere with yourself! Then and only then can you be honest and sincere with your fellowman.

What is honesty? Honesty is truthfulness. What is sincerity? Sincerity is authentic or genuine. In order to understand self, we must understand the concept of honesty and sincerity.

SELF EVALUATION

Some of the common questions to self include "What's wrong with my thinking? Why do I feel I am not worthy as a person? Why do I exist? Why do I feel like my power has been depleted? Why is my desire to achieve gone? Do past failures cloud my future? Has the loss of a child or family member pushed me over the edge?"

"What's wrong with my thinking? Has rejection or exclusion been a part of my on going experience?" (Family, friends, co-workers, other relationships)

Do you have a fear that something bad is going to happen, fear of not living up to what others expect, fear of not being good enough, fear of death or fear of being alone?

What's wrong with my thinking? Could it be that things that happened to you as a child have carried over to your adult life? (Lack of attention, physical abuse, sexual abuse, mental or verbal abuse).

What are your addictions: drugs, alcohol, food, sex, pornography, or gossip?

These are band aids that cover-up our underlying problems of low self-esteem, fear, unworthiness, feeling of depleted power, past failures, personal losses, and abuse.

Ask yourself the following questions:

How do I feel about myself?

Where do these feelings come from?

How long have I had these feelings?

Who are the people that have impacted my life in a negative way?   (Individuals, groups, family, friends, co-workers, classmates, etc.)

What is your greatest fear?

Did it come as a child or adult?

Who put it there?

List all the health problems you had as a child or adult.

Do you feel a need to make people feel you are something that you are not just to be accepted?

Are you a yes person?

Do you or did you have a good relationship with your parents?
Are you from a single parent home?

If so, what was your situation like?

What are some of things you faced living at home with one parent?

Did you get all the attention you felt you needed?
Were you alone a lot? What kind of relationship did you have with your parent or guardian? What was positive and what was negative about being raised by one parent?

How did you get along with your siblings?
Did you communicate together on a regular basis? Was there respect for each other? Were you treated differently?

How did your parents handle their problems in the home?
Did they work through their conflicts? Did their communication fail and then fighting started?

How did it affect you?
Did that behavior carry over to your adult life? Is it affecting your family now?

Are you teaching your children to behave differently than the way you were raised?

Do you feel this change is positive?

There are so many reasons why one might lose their drive for life, but one of the most powerful negatives that destroys more lives than anything else is the tongue (talk)! When a person speaks, he or she can speak life or death to the hearer. Whether the words are to a child, wife, husband, girl friend, boy friend, sister, brother etc., they can be deadly.

The success or failure of many children was determined early in their childhood. Think about these words, "You never will be anything. You are just like your no good father. Why are you so dumb? Can't you do anything right? I hate you." These words cut very deep and have a long-term effect, sometimes for life. Life and death is in the power of what you say.

We all must look at where we came from to see and understand where we are going. If we find that where we came from is affecting where we are going, then we must make the commitment to change.

LESSON IN SELF ESTEEM

Self-esteem issues occur when you accept what others have to say about how you look, talk, walk, think and/or act. We want to be accepted so badly that we take everything negative about us to heart and then we turn inwardly and attack our self, our worth, and our purpose for existing.

Our self-esteem issues occur early in our life. The negative things people say to you as a child and teen affect how you feel about yourself as an adult. Without early intervention and a strong support element, self-esteem can become a major issue in your life and the lives of those you come in contact with. You must be honest with your feelings to begin to change how you think and feel about yourself. Remember our children's lives are affected and everyone else we love.

SELF CONFIDENCE

You were born to be victorious! The very first step in cultivating self-confidence is to learn to rely on your own physical, mental and spiritual strengths. It is entirely a matter of getting to know your self more completely. You have to discover what your own natural abilities and possibilities really are.

Then you must learn to depend on your natural strengths in every detail of your private life. Self-confidence must germinate and grow within you, if you want it to be a lasting quality. Other people may help you in certain ways, from time to time, but the way to permanent success is to rely upon your own inner resources!

The word "confidence" means a sincere belief in something. It means a positive, courageous "faith" that is based upon understanding. Self-confidence is self-faith. It has been proven that we cannot think of two different ideas at the same time. If we develop a faith in ourselves, we automatically lose all fear and uncertainty regarding ourselves.

This is imperative. You must once and for all, drive out of your mind every sort of fear, doubt and hesitation. The way to do that is by the following technique.

THINK POWER-GENERATING THOUGHTS

Impress your subconscious mind with thoughts of strength, personal courage and the will to achieve. Affirm self-confidence until it becomes an automatic reflex. Think about your good qualities and accent them. Resolve to build up the qualities you now lack. Be true to yourself. Self-confidence must exist in your own mind before you can express it outwardly with genuine conviction. Inwardly, you must first convince yourself that you actually are a dynamic, confident person. It does no good to "play-act" the part, if you really don't believe it is true.

That is just kidding your self! People are very quick to catch on to pretense of any kind, and nobody likes insincerity. All that is really necessary to become self-confident is to have a genuine appreciation of your positive qualities. Everyone has greater possibilities than he or she can as yet imagine. Wake up to the good that is in you right now. Bless and praise it until those around you recognize it. Rely on your strengths without doubt.

Don't plan the impossible. Self-confidence cannot grow on false pretenses. We must never waste valuable time in planning impossible things, that is, things too far removed from the world of practical reality. If we try to accomplish too much at one time, the inevitable result is that we disappoint ourselves by scattering our forces unsuccessfully. It is very important to your mind to use good judgment as we advance in life. Remember to keep a personal control over your ambitions. First succeed in small things, and do not over extend yourself.

All timidity should be overcome. Banish shyness and timidity. The timid person cannot appear natural. He or she will appear stiff, cold, reserved, and yet can be just the opposite. Shy people never have much magnetism because of their retiring nature.

They continually put off what should be done at once. In this way they lose many opportunities they might have grasped. You cannot take your rightful place in life until you have conquered your shyness. You will find it a little difficult at first, but every time you conquer yourself when you notice a tendency to shrink from something you should do, you will find it easier the next time.

Shyness and timidity are purely mental characteristics. Most of it is caused by imagination. When a person is shy he thinks that whatever he does or says, someone is looking at him or listening to him. If you are timid, try the following technique: No matter what you are doing, never look around to see if someone is watching you. Whatever you have to do go ahead and do it immediately. Never think whether you are being watched or not. Put all your attention on what you are doing!

Be self-determined. This means to be a "self-starter". Rely on your own mental and physical resources and make use of them at every opportunity. Never wait for "lady luck" to smile on you, but use your brain–that is your Mind Power–and your two strong arms to attain what you desire. What you do not use, you lose, so put your good traits and positive qualities into active use now, and keep on developing them. A natural "chain-reaction" will follow your action when you start with real energy and enthusiasm.

Fortunes have been built on this principle of starting with enthusiastic energy. The big secret of rising in the world is to apply the power of your positive emotions as a "spark" to release the physical energy you need to accomplish things. Most people wait to be "cranked" into action. You can far outdistance them by using emotional-power to "start" yourself!

William James, famous psychologist, once said, "No creature is born timid. Look at the naturalness of all animals. Human beings are made timid by suggestions from external sources—people or things. These suggestions literally make the individual 'conscious of self' and there his troubles begin."

Spontaneity, one of the most attractive qualities, is impossible to the man who is conscious of himself. His mind is always turned inward upon himself instead of upon the thing he is trying to do. Consequently, he never does it effectively.

The Law of Suggestion is simply this: you tend to follow every suggestion made to you, unless inhibited by a stronger suggestion in another direction. Every action you perform is, directly or indirectly, the result of a suggestion from something or somebody. Unfortunately, adequacy and inferiority are made so by parents or others with whom you grow up.

The child is literally bombarded with negative suggestions from well-meaning, but uniformed parents, who tell him that he is "too young" or "too little" to do this or that. The idea of fear is easily instilled in the impressionable subconscious mind of a child, and many parents use this fear as a means of disciplining their children. This fear-pattern often persists throughout life.

We know that suggestion of a negative kind can make you self-conscious depending upon how sensitive and impressionable you are. By the same token, we know that you can use the Law of Suggestion in a positive way - we can reverse the effect.

Many people condemn and criticize themselves, unmercifully; little faults are magnified into big faults, by repeating them. Don't continually talk about your faults or shortcomings to others. Don't depreciate yourself. Every time you do you tend to impress those things more deeply in your subconscious mind. This amounts to negative self-suggestion.

Instead of apologizing or blushing when people give you compliments or praise, say "Thank you" and accept them. You must learn the good about you and get every doubt about your ability out of your system once and for all. After all, how do you know you can't do something---anything--- until you try?

You are not a victim of "chance" or "fate" or "circumstances" except as you think you are. When you think you are beaten, you are. When you think failure, your own fear-thought is fashioning the conditions for failure. There is only one antidote for this kind of fear thinking.

We call it the "Direct Action Technique".

The idea is to first say to your self, "I can and I will!" and then go into action without further ado. Approach whatever life problem is confronting you, regardless of what it is—a business decision, making a sale, buying a new hat - etc, -- and quickly list all the different solutions you can think of. Select the solution that seems to be the best, and do everything necessary to apply that solution. If you don't obtain the results you desire, apply the other solutions, one by one.

People want you to be original, that is, your own natural self, not necessarily like themselves. The psychology of this is simply that we all like to be stimulated by new and different personalities, not the same ones all the time. When trying to display your own personality, be sure it is really you and not somebody else you are trying to display. Develop your own personality into the sparkling asset it can and should be and avoid any imitation of others. Real sincerity is vitally essential. Wearing a "false mask" will cause you to be self-conscious.

The next time you meet somebody, or face a new situation, act out your real, original self. If you will do this, you will not appear shy or timid, but at ease and self-confident. You see, your real self does not know the meaning of failure or fear, but you've got to step aside and let it express itself naturally.

Timid individuals may be fine, sensitive people, however, their very sensitivity causes them to suffer mentally whenever they imagine themselves left out or neglected by others. Timidity inspires no one.

In psychology, three basic personality types are recognized.

The Introvert, who is more concerned with what is happening within his mind, than what is occurring in the world about him. He (or she) is acutely aware of his own feelings and reactions, hence is overly conscious of self, sometimes to the point of extreme timidity; avoids people.

The Extrovert is the "natural born salesperson" type. He (or she) is not completely happy unless mingling with people, talking with them and trying to convince them of one thing or another. The extrovert will stop work anytime for a cup of coffee, just for the chance of expressing his ideas to someone else. He is much more interested in what is going on in the world around him than what his own thoughts and feelings might be.

The Ambivert is a combination of the qualities and traits of both the Introvert and Extrovert. In other words, the Ambivert is a thinker as will as a doer; hence he (or she) is not overly sensitive nor does he try to cram his personal opinions down your throat. He has a dynamic, balanced approach to life.

Fear is at the root of all timidity. The old gospel of self-effacing humility has been over-sold. The real virtue lies in getting honest with you, and acting like one of God's creations, instead of trying to be like a worm of the dust. You were created for dominion; timidity is not for a king. Nor is it the natural role of a queen.

Timid people have a strong desire to help humanity, but their very timidity places two strikes against them from the start. Did you ever see a timid man inspire anyone to do anything great? Nobody respects the weakling. Instead, people step on him. But let a self-confident individual say or do something, and the whole world listens in admiration. Human beings are like that.

One of the greatest secrets of building self-confidence is this: Be a "Go Giver" rather than a "Go-Getter". You have been taught for years to struggle and strain and sweat to "get things", and "do things" but that is not the right psychology to follow.

When you accent the idea of "getting", it automatically puts a big barrier in your way. Your thoughts turn inward upon yourself making you self-conscious. But when we learn to accent the idea of giving, the mind turns outward towards the recipient of our gift. This state of mind makes us self-confident, because it takes our thoughts away from self. It stands to reason that this attitude will bring happiness.

Developing confidence in yourself and your abilities is not a difficult task, but it does require patience and persistence. Other people are not as conscious of you as you imagine. They are busy with their own troubles. Rather than thinking of you, they are usually wondering what you are thinking about them. Remember, it is in your power to change the slide of mental pictures in your own mind. Control your thinking. Keep a positive picture there and it will come true.

DREAMS ARE REALITIES

Your dreams can become a reality, whether it is for riches, power, tranquility, or a baby girl born to fulfill a dream for a first-born.

Dreams can be reality. They must be put into conscious thought before they can become reality. The physical form of thought takes physical action, which is guided by thought and it then becomes reality.

There has never been a question that has entered your mind that you cannot go to the same source and get the answer. The mind cannot ask a question that it can't answer. You have to delve very deep within and find true sources to get all of this answer, but the answers are there. Go to the source.

We know thought exists, but we cannot see thought. The channel of the mind is the same way. You are what you think and you must think properly if you want to accomplish anything in life. Life is what you make it -- heaven or hell. Know what you want before you put your mind into thought and allow it to happen. If you think it with strong belief, it will happen. Make sure you want to live with it before you create it.

You are somebody special and important. You are a force in life. Who you are counts.

You must break the old cycle of negative thinking. How you view life is how you live life. Love the person that God created you to be. The feeling of "I am a failure" is a deception, and can be over come with time and effort.

Self-evaluation, realization an affirmation,
commitment and persistence will carry you along way.

Self-Evaluation

Realistically look at your life and your environment.
Look at the past and present, the positives and the
negatives.   Understand what you must do.   Realize
and affirm "I am human and sensitive.   I have allowed
others to affect my life.   I have been my worst enemy.
I will change how I feel about myself.   I will love and
respect myself. I understand what I want my outcome
to be."

DESIRE

In order to accomplish what you desire, you must continually be on guard against holding negative mental pictures in your mind. You've got to keep your mind filled with 100% constructive thoughts at all times. Intensify the right desires. Your mind has to work for you and not against you. Fill your mind with positive mental pictures or visualizations of yourself doing the thing you desire to do! This principle of Mental-Picturing will add oil to the flame of your desire. You'll be impelled from within to do every thing within your power, to realize your right desires!

Know exactly what you desire. Be specific about what you desire. You can have anything in this world, within limits of course, if only you know exactly what it is you want. Now here is a helpful suggestion: It is important that you learn to think ahead regarding the logical outcome of the action you plan to take. If the final outcome of it appears to benefit you, and not interfere with your personal progress in any way, go ahead and decide to do that thing. When you are sure this is the thing you want to do, make up your mind that "the die is cast." Clinch your mind and lock it up! Don't change your mind the very next moment, and be continually "on the fence." Think first. Consider carefully, go ahead, and follow through!

There is within you a mighty, irresistible power with which you can perform tasks almost beyond belief. It is not an imaginary power, but a very real one and you can use it, if only you will. You can, if you must. This power is the reserve energy of your deeper mind; the subconscious wherein lies your real strength. You've got to tap that great reserve of energy in your subconscious, and compel that energy to give you keener, greater, and more sustained powers of mind and body! No matter what you want to achieve or acquire and no matter what your line of work is you can use this principle of reserve energy to succeed!

Here is how to apply this great principle of success. Tell yourself you must accomplish what you desire to do. This is an emergency and you must attain your objective. Actually it really is an emergency, for unless you bring your willpower into action, and start moving toward your goal, you will never reach it. So make your own emergency, right now. Affirm to yourself over and over, I can and I will! Plunge in! Start now!

Your conscious Mind is your "decider." Once you make a decision, turn the job over to your subconscious mind and demand new supplies of mental and physical energy to work for you.

Wake up your will to win! Why would you run in low gear when you can run in high gear just as easily? The amazing truth is that it will tire you less to work at high pitch than it does to drag along on surface energy. Don't be afraid to drive yourself to work faster and accomplish big things. It will not hurt you, provided you get your proper amount of rest and relaxation. The idea is to get the new pattern started by conscious effort, which means positive thinking and decision. Quicken your pace by drawing upon your vast reserves of energy. Keep your mind filled with mental pictures of how you will benefit from getting the thing you are working for. This inspires you to win!

Your will power can be developed both consciously and subconsciously. The conscious mind is the decider whereas the subconscious is the doer or the power behind your will that gets things done. Both of these parts of your mind should be developed in harmony for greatest personal power. This is the basis of a dynamic will. Will is bound to show itself in your face and manner even though you may not realize it. Nothing will encourage you more and nothing will prove to you your own power of will, like compelling yourself to do something disagreeable. Any weakling can take the path of least resistance and do things he likes to do; pleasant easy, agreeable things, but these do not make the will stronger.

Every day do something you do not like to do. Make up your mind to do it just for the purpose of accomplishment. Do not slow your progress and waste time doing impractical things, but make the things you do boost you further toward success. Use all the consciousness of will power you have been storing and don't give up. Each time you succeed, you are much stronger than before.

The positive mental pictures you build in your mind make a deep impression upon the deeper part of mind known as your subconscious.

They act to direct the subconscious to create for you the kind of conditions in your life that boost you ahead! Therefore, your mental attitude consciously must be made up of two ideas; I can, I will, and how.

If you will constantly hold this attitude you will accomplish with ease what you formerly considered far beyond the realm of possibility for you.

You will draw from your subconscious mind the precise plans and power for actually doing the impossible. This is the right use of your subconscious mind.

Remember, the resolute action of your will can move heaven and earth to get you what you truly desire--- because the union of will and desire makes an irresistible team in action!

Mark 11:24   Therefore I say unto you, What things so ever ye desire, when ye pray, believe that ye receive them, and ye shall have them.

THE WILL

A newborn baby's first cry announces the birth of willpower. A baby cries due to discomfort and for the activity of his lungs. This is called "automatic physiological volition." When the baby grows old enough to talk, and unquestioningly follows the wishes of his mother. It is said to possess "unthinking will." Then the baby grows older and begins to think for himself: the baby is now using the next step of evolving will. This stage is termed "blind will" because it is not guided by wisdom. Many young people use this explosive blind will without any useful purpose, wasting energy and higher possibilities on passions, temptations, fighting, ungoverned appetites and so forth.

A "thinking will" is a realization of a blind will. After experiencing its' results, the youth learn what is meant by "thinking will". Even thinking will become ineffective, however, if used too much in wrong activities. But if one's thinking will retains its normal power and is made to revolve around a definite purpose, it becomes "dynamic will." Such will should be used for a wholesome purpose; actions in tune with universal harmony strengthen the will and lead to success.

A wrongly used will weakens itself because of a lack of encouragement from truth and is out of tune with universal order. When one knows that his objective or the nature of his purpose is worthwhile, then the tenacity of his volition becomes greater.

You are now prepared mentally for specific techniques by which you may build your power of will, and direct your destiny.

Recognize your own power!   Before you can ever build a dynamic will, you have to first come to an inner realization that you have a will-- that is, the power of deciding what you desire to do or acquire! This power of your mind must be awakened and developed by active use.

It is highly essential to realize that the real you is not your outer form or personality, not your weaker self, but the "ego" which is the real 'I' within you.

When you consciously will to do a certain thing, your real self instantly begins to release powers into your life which give you new strength and ambition. Inner resources, in which you previously had little confidence, begin to make themselves available to assist your purpose.

One must use dynamic power of will to fight for truth until success comes. A strong will creates a way for its own fulfillment by its very strength.

The will sets into motion vibrations in the atmosphere and nature. A strong will always finds a way.   For absolute control of your life and in order to destroy root-causes of failure, you must exercise your will in every undertaking.

Willpower is endurance and determination!

Will power is not merely a matter of thinking. It is thinking plus feeling. Thoughts are cold, but feelings are warm, alive, and vital. What we call will is in reality directed desire.

The first principle in building a powerful will is to learn to desire what you know is beneficial and good for you. Naturally, we are not concerned with the use of desire for purposes of a negative nature. You can use this power to boost you forward in life, or drag you down, as you prefer. But when desire is rightly directed, your personal advancement is greatly speeded up.

Wishes never got anyone very far in life. You must not only wish, you must desire with a powerful, unyielding intensity. You must awaken into positive activity all the powers of your body, mind and soul, if you will make real progress in getting those good and worthwhile things of life!

Many people in the world are like sheep, rabbits or meek turtle doves who have never known what it means to be filled with a tremendous, positive desire that can move mountains if need be. They sit meekly, too self-effacing to ever demand what they want from life. Instead, they let the strong-minded ones, those who are compelled by strong desires, gather up the good things and accomplish the great things in life. This is why so many fail and so few succeed. Will power or more precisely, "Desire-Power" is sadly lacking in the average person's makeup in this day and age, and has been lacking for a long time.

A friend said, "I have brought myself, after long meditation, to the conviction that a human being with a definite purpose can accomplish it. Nothing can resist a will which will stake existence, if need be, on its fulfillment!" That is the kind of will power that can open the door to anything you want out of life. You can build that kind of will power if you learn how to stir up your desire. You've got to put the power of your emotional nature behind your thoughts. Only the energy releasing power of your emotions can push your body into dynamic action.

Remember that thoughts and decisions have to be supported by physical action for results. You've got to first decide what to do, determine that you will do it, and then act! Others have succeeded in the very things you desire to do, and so can you, if you try!

YOUR GREATEST ENEMY HABITS

Most likely your present habits, or at least a number of them, are enemy habits. However, if you faithfully apply the principles of this course, your habits will change from negative to positive and become your best friends.

Actually, your habits are simply a matter of past conditioning from your environment and way of living. You know which habits are boosting your progress and which are hindering it. After you have made up your mind that your personal progress is vastly more important than undesirable habits, it will be easy to break the old patterns and establish new ones.

Do not try to destroy your bad habits by force. The secret is simply to replace the bad habits with good habits. Make the good ones strong enough and they will automatically destroy the others. Don't try to change yourself in a single day. Start in the right direction and persist until you arrive at your destination.

COMMITMENT

I will overcome my fears and doubts. I will work toward change. I will love myself. I will honor my life.

THE GREAT POWER OF PERSISTENCE

Apply consistent effort into changing, and stick with it until your transformation is complete. See it through. Persistence takes us to the desired outcome. There are millions of "starters" in this world—persons who get excited and enthusiastic about something, and start out toward it but never reach it.

They fizzle out long before the goal is attained. They lack the power of persistence.

You can overdo persistence by carrying it to the point of stubbornness, but realizing this, it is not likely that you will. The person of most effective will power is not he who clenches his teeth, tenses his muscles, scowls fiercely and goes at his task with brutish force. He may succeed, but he is wasting energy and rapidly exhausting his energy and enthusiasm. That is why he will probably "fizzle out" before too long. He is "bee-fighting", which means his energy is applied in the wrong direction. Instead of fighting, he needs to learn how to cooperate with others, and stick to the job until it is accomplished.

To develop persistence, learn to be thorough in what you do. Keep your mind centered on what you are trying to accomplish. Take pride in performing your job to the best of your abilities. Stir up your desire to do it now and do it right.

Project yourself out of careless, indifferent or slipshod habits of working, by developing greater pride in your work. Stick to it until it is done right.

Persistence will grant you achievement in anything you desire by fully developing your creative mind and using your creative forces. Endurance and determination will open the door to even greater wisdom, which will allow you to achieve what you pursue in life.

To be happy materially can lead you to be happy mentally. To be happy mentally allows you to have the time and peace of mind to develop spiritually, which in turn will allow true happiness in your own development. Dreams are realities, and realities are words with modification put behind them. Words are power!

MATERIAL GAIN

"The nature of man is to own and possess. To understand life is to have great success. To have all the comfort, of material gain, is the law of nature and man's first aim."

No matter what road we take, our ultimate goal is happiness! Happiness means something different to every person in the world! Happiness is a state of mind, and the most important aspect of happiness is perfection in everything you attempt in life! Happiness is a true friendship through trust! Happiness is when we are on the pursuit and capture of truth! Happiness is earned! Happiness is "to get out of life what you put into it" attitude! No limit is put upon man except what man puts upon himself.

If man's hunger for knowledge is great and he searches for truth and sincerity, and gains wisdom, there is no limit to his attainment in life. Man must search for self-reliance, dig deep for attaining knowledge and understand the universe as a whole. Man must join the occupation of seeking happiness so that he may realize that happiness lies in happiness itself. Man's happiness is understanding himself and the things around him.

You are your own master for material gain, grasp it and grow. This is your chance for fame. Life's destinies hold many ups and downs; you must take it all without a frown. You have the abilities to make things nice for you. Know your ingredients well, put in the right spice; each spice is different. Many flavors will unfold. Taste them all, set your own table, and enjoy your own feast! Whether you desire a mansion or a simple place, live life well and above all, run your best race.

Let us discuss how we draw success to us on all levels. The basic formula is the same, whether it is large or small in fame or material gain. Success is not luck or a by-chance happening. There is a basic formula that must be applied and practiced. Let us discuss some of the basic rules of success. The five "W's", who, what, when, where, why (and sometimes how) represent an important analysis of any course. Who is the person working on the project? Where is the destiny of the finished product? What is the course you will take? Why will you do this? How will it be accomplished?

Analyze all things that you desire. Know the material resources that are at your fingertips. Apply the five "w's" to each object you wish to obtain. You now have a goal and you now have created the desire. The next step is to create a plan for attaining the desired goal. Let your forces work for you, not against you. Believe! Now, allow your desire to come forth. The power of the mind can build or destroy. Utilize all your sources and realize words are power.

The secret to success is positive thoughts. Take the word desire, for instance. Desire is to want. To want means that you must place your desire in your mind so strong that it becomes a part of you. Desire to win; desire to gain. The desire must be a part of your very being in order to have success. When you have the desire strong enough and combine it with the strength of your thoughts, you will obtain your goal. Never allow anyone or anything to stand in your way once you have put your plan in motion. Anyone can obtain any goal if the desire is strong enough to motivate you to action.

Three words of power that you must incorporate into your vocabulary are ...

Understand - to comprehend, to know how and have full knowledge on the subject matter. Let us understand what we desire and why it is needed. What will it take to receive my desire? Where is it coming from? Understand what is positive and negative about your desire. Understand what you must sacrifice to achieve your goal. Be willing to accept the path ahead. Now that you understand, you are ready for action. By creating a strong desire, and understanding the negative and positive forces surrounding the desire, you can continue to strive until you succeed. By all means, get to the tasks at hand and enjoy the process to attaining your personal goal.

Endure - persevere, persist, continue, stand under adverse circumstances.

When we want to succeed we must have the physical and mental endurance to see our project through. There have been times in your life, and there will be more times in your life, when you have felt that there was a brick wall in front of you and you could see no way of getting over, around, or through this mammoth wall. This is when you will need the power of endurance. If you can remove but one brick a day, eventually the wall will be down. If you have the endurance to see it through you will succeed. You will always win if you continue through your entire project keeping your desire strong and your willingness to sacrifice to obtain your goal.

Faith - assurance, trust, credence, sureness.

It is very important to have faith in one's self, your fellowman, and the goal you wish to obtain. The word faith is what our entire universe is based upon. Have faith in the Master who rules our entire universe. He will help you to succeed. Have faith that you can control your emotions and your responses to the upheavals in life. Tune in to the laws of the universe. By exercising faith, you can accomplish anything. When you have faith in what you have set out to accomplish or obtain, it makes the entire project become a reality, you are mentally ready to receive what you have striven for.

There has not been anything in my life that I have truly wanted, that I could not create the desire strong enough to receive it. I say this so you can realize that anyone can accomplish their desire if motivated properly. You must utilize every source within your body, mind and soul.

All of the sources can be tapped. They will be there when you need them. You must have understanding, endurance, and faith to reach these higher forces. You can, and will with the proper amount of time, patience, and practice. Once you have made contact with your higher forces, you can bring them into use in your everyday life. This force will protect, teach and bring thoughts to you. You will have developed your mind into something beautiful, positive, powerful, and useful!

The laws of nature have an unusual way of allowing information to come to us. Always be open to new suggestions. Be able to understand the forces involved in your project. Allow them to join in creating what you desire. Your enthusiasm should be catching to all those that are around you. The secrets are all there. Application is a necessity to succeed. Become very keen and alert to the word opportunity. You must be willing to accept change when one plan fails. You must accept the changes with eagerness and zest.

Opportunities are around us every day of our lives. We can't recognize them unless we are aware. Listen to the meaning behind each word spoken, not just to the word itself; observe what is being expressed. Understand by body language, understand by context, and understand by tone. Understand what the person is trying to convey to you. When you listen and watch carefully, the person you are conversing with can be motivated by your desire. This is how some opportunities are found and magnetically pulled to provide creative and financial help for your project.

Concentrate deeply on the meanings, the expressions of speech, and physical reactions. This will guide you to knowing what must be applied to motivate the entirety of this person. Look for the opportunity in the voice regarding the subject matter you are discussing. See the interest. If there is none, create it. Once you have created the interest in the person, you will know what is available from this person. Realize what part you want this person to play in the success of your project. This will give you immediate help toward your goal.

When there is no interest and you cannot create interest, or motivate the person you have chosen to share your creation with, don't waste time. Go on to the next person that you have decided to share your dream with. The blessing and support is far greater with someone with whom you can connect.

Always remember you created your goal; it was worthwhile for you to invest your time into it. It will only be a matter of time until you find the person that has that same enthusiasm you hold for your project.

Know there is opportunity and it's always knocking at the door of your subconscious mind. Listen constantly and carefully, and it will never steer you wrong. It is up to you to tap the source by keeping your mind clear of all negative thoughts.

The word confidence is another very important word and should become a part of your very existence. Do not confuse this word with egotism. Confidence should begin in yourself as a human being - one of the highest orders of the universe. Have confidence in your very being, confidence in what you desire and confidence that you will receive it. Confidence that you have obtained all knowledge surrounding the project and confidence that you have endurance to reach the goal you have set.

We must have confidence especially when things look bleak. Have confidence that you will succeed in whatever you take upon yourself to obtain and it will remain through faith and the positive mind that you now possess.

When a change must be made to ensure our success, have faith in that change. Keep the confidence in the opportunity that has been given you and do not destroy it with greed or other negative forces. Your words and conduct must be honorable and honest to succeed.

Negative thoughts will eventually destroy you. Remain with a clean, honest and positive thought toward yourself and your fellow man. The person who cheats finds success is a very short-lived affair and eventually destroys himself though his own vicious and greedy mind. The opportunity given you through your search for the truth has opened your mind to greater things in life than becoming involved with the unfruitful negative things and people that exist in our world today.

Understand the greatness that can come to you by the positive thoughts you allow you to dwell within your mind. Search out and destroy all the negative thoughts that you may still harbor within the foundation of your being. Realize they are made up of destructive devices and will eventually destroy you, those you love, and your possessions.

When you find a depressed mood coming upon you, realize that depression can destroy your very being. Immediately dismiss the negative thought and replace it with a positive thought. When you have accomplished this one time, the second time becomes easier, and soon you will have developed the powerful habit of positive thought.

We are all creatures of habit, release the bad ones and send them on their way. Replace them with a good, strong, positive thought and become the master of your own mind. You are just as capable as the greatest person you have ever admired. With determination and knowledge, you can accomplish some of the same things you admire (not envy) in someone else. You may even become better than the pattern that you have chosen to follow.

One of the most moving expressions that a successful person will use is, "I will do it". If you listen closely you will hear the determination in the tone of the voice. This is an example of will power and can show the will to do and the power to follow it through. I am not speaking to the person who is afraid, I'm speaking to the person who will do whatever positive thing is necessary to succeed.

"I will do" is a much stronger phrase than "Maybe I will do." Notice the reaction that comes over your mental state as you think about these two responses. The positive thought makes you feel elated and sure that there will be action; mentally you are waiting on the next movement to motivate you into action. The negative remark, "Maybe I will" has a tendency to make you irritable and physically tired and brings on an argumentative mood of depression which comes from indecision.

A person feels secure with decision, and can relax the mind and allow it to move on to the next step at hand. Indecision keeps a person at a stand still. Frustration sets in and causes decay of the mind and laziness of the body, and eventually causes destruction. Realizing the destruction that you can bring on yourself through negative thoughts, let's now erase the negativity from our life and save the beauty of positive effect around us from now on. By not allowing negative thoughts to stay in your mind again, you will accomplish your desires. No matter how hopeless a task may seem, you will better understand that it is always darkest just before the dawn.

Keep your goal in mind and have confidence that you will succeed. There is no one in this world that can stop you from obtaining the desire you wish, except you! You, alone, know and understand the true desires that you are creating; you alone can win or lose; it's all in the way you think. The power to follow through on the best-laid plans comes from the determination in your own mind. Utilize all of your God-given talents and develop them fully.

When you reach out to receive your standard in life, you must reach out with enthusiasm and zest. You must really understand where you are going. Understand who you are and what destination you choose. Ponder this well before you proceed any further. Are you a negative thinking person? Are you a positive thinking person? Can you make a decision and be convicted in your stand? If you are a positive thinking person, then you understand what will take place with each step toward your goal. You understand how to make a decision when the proper time arises. It all begins with thought. Nourish and cherish your thoughts and watch them grow. With positive thought and good will to your fellow man, you will succeed.

Life has many ups and downs; many individual battles. Testimonials can be heard everywhere. We must remain positive. By thinking positive, we think properly. This is the only way that we can curtail any negativity that we must face from our associates and friends. Once we understand the difference in a positive and a negative thought, we can bring our "downs" or failures to a minimum. When we have understanding, we can control our destiny. We can control our environment. This does not mean in a dogmatic fashion! This means that we understand that we control our responses to the events that take place in our life, and that our responses shape our environment. Once we control our emotions and use energy forces properly, we now control our destination and our success for the material or emotional goals we have set out to accomplish.

Henry Ford created and developed an empire. There have been many positive and negative thoughts that have been expressed about this gentleman, but never the less, he was successful in his endeavor for a financial empire.   Henry Ford was one of the great creative minds of our times.   His desire was for success; his method to obtain his desired goal was transportation. This man's education was limited. His creative powers were limitless. Henry Ford thought strong and positive.   Negative thoughts did not become a part of this man. He developed the ability for great earning capacity in the field of transportation, with creative forces for material gain far beyond anyone's wildest dreams at that time. Today, the car has become every teenage boy's dream to possess, every adult's necessity and a way of life that would be hard to exist without.

Henry Ford's desire became so strong that it created the will which motivated his imagination.   He was without formal education but blessed with the knowledge of the sources to tap and the burning desire to create. He seemed to know within himself from the beginning that all he had to do was to think it and he could accomplish it.

Eventually he was able to buy the long box of buttons that sat on his desk. Behind each button with a mere press from his finger, he immediately had his five W's at his fingertips in the names of engineers, bookkeepers, secretaries, etc.   They brought the mechanics of the project to him. He did not need this type of knowledge stored in his head.   The buttons would suffice.   He had the key to all of their successes through the power to create. The creation is the most important factor here.   Without the creation, there would be no need for the buttons.

This food for thought is to ask the question, "Are you the creative mind or are you a button on someone's desk?" If you are that button or number, then take a good look at yourself. Creation comes in many forms. Analyze the most important person you are going to improve: you. Use your own creative ability in your chosen field. Live the exciting life you were meant to live. Don't settle for mere existence in the seventy or eighty years that you have been allotted.

What do you want? What does what you want represent? What type of home and environment do you want? Now, if you want love and happiness, please remember that this particular chapter is about material gain, not emotional stability. That comes later.   The emotional stability we will discuss does involve your physical welfare. If you are not satisfied with the money you now possess and want more then we have a small matter to contend with. Money can come to you as though you were a magnet. You put the positive thoughts in control, allowing the creative forces to come forward into your mind. They will bring more ideas than you could have imagined!

You now have a decision to make in choosing the best idea and creating it to the fullest capacity. Let's put into practice our motivation and get going on our research to gain all known information on the subject matter at hand. Once we have this knowledge from publications, discussions, documentaries, etc., we can now delve into our own creative forces again and come up with the new application and revelation that we will receive from our creative forces.   Listen well and you can hear the answers coming to you.   Your magnetic forces are now working in force with your enthusiasm and faith, the material gain will come.

Money is one of the easiest commodities we receive in life. Remember, money is only an exchange set up by man to purchase the items to make his life more comfortable while he remains in the physical body. I want you to understand the value of money and what its purpose really is in your life.   Try this exercise. Close your eyes for a second and visualize yourself far above the earth you are now living upon. See this in your mind clearly -- a very small earth, about the size of a baseball.   This puts you away from your problem at hand so you may see the entire picture. When you are looking at your small earth, ask yourself this question: What does it take to survive on the planet below? The answer is money.   Set your standard of living at this very moment.   At this very moment, you decide exactly what you want to do to obtain the money that your standard of living requires. Do not dismiss ideas that you may think foolish.

Now that you realize that all of your ideas are food for thought,   carefully   analyze   all   your   creative impressions.   Select your choice and see yourself in possession of the very thing that your inner sources have shown you.   See yourself using it, see yourself living with it. See yourself already in possession of it. It is yours. The material resources to obtain it will be there. When you are in need of a certain amount of money, write the exact amount on a large card that is placed where you can see it at all times. Place it in your plain view, where it can be photographed by your mind.

Concentrate so deeply on this figure that you will know it will be there and it is yours. See yourself in possession of the desired amount. See yourself in possession of the goal you have set for yourself, living with it, owning it.

See yourself using it. Keep this thought until you obtain it. Do not change your thought to another desire or goal until you have accomplished this one. When you split your energies, there are not as strong as when you apply your full mental energies toward one goal.

If it is the money that you have chosen as your first project or goal, use this as a rule. Write down on a piece of paper, the object you wish to receive. Place this paper where you can constantly see it. Write it again every night before you fall asleep. Do this until you can see it in your mind. See the object, see your possession, touch it, feel it, taste it, and above all know it is yours. With this method, you will see it come to you very quickly. With this positive thought and physical move, you will magnetically pull all opportunities to you.

The power of concentration is a very strong force. You are actually sending thoughts into the universe and there will be a receiver around someplace that will pick these thoughts up. So, keep them very positive for help to yourself and your fellowman. With these good thoughts placed openly into the universe and if the thoughts are consistent, someone will hear your desire and help you in some unforeseen way, either in a physical form or spiritual.

Everyone has spiritual guidance whether they utilize it or not. It is still there. Ask and you shall receive. See it mentally and you own it. Touch it, and it is in your possession. Think positive and you will bring it to you.

Never doubt your abilities. Anything you desire in life, search for it and know your subject matter inside out, realize and know everything it stands for. It is a life you created; breathe into it and make it mean something. This way you make it have merit and it will be strong enough to stand on its own. Once your desires are put into form, it lives.

Dreams come from thoughts and thoughts become reality. You created it, you put life into it with your work, and you breathed the very life into it that makes it exist. Without you, it would have never become a reality. Your creator did such a fantastic job on you that once you see this, you will realize He put everything here for you to work with. Tap your hidden sources, send the message positive and strong for what you desire, your resources are here.

There will be times in your life that the decision that you have made has been the wrong one. You may ask if the mistakes are lack of thought placed around the goal. Once you have determined that what you thought to pursue is a mistake, realize that the process of its pursuit, will be one of the greatest teachers you will ever have. One of the common causes of failure is giving up too soon. Sometimes we are too quick to call it a mistake, give up and go on to something else.

We must examine the event, and if a mistake has truly been made, we must rectify the mistake before we move on to another project. It is very important to rectify the error through research. When we have found the cause of the mistake, we can correct it and turn the project into a success.

Remember, we are creatures of habit. Once we set the pattern for following through on all of our projects, we have created the habit of winning. When we do not finish the project at hand and give up, this makes us a loser and this can also become a habit. Make yourself a winner by finishing every project that you start. When you have made a mistake, don't let it get you down. Pick yourself up and return to the cause at hand. You can find an immediate solution to your mistake and rectify it. The lesson you learn from mistakes should never be forgotten.

One thought to recall about a mistake is that it was your mistake; you created it and you have the power to destroy it. The main thought that you must receive out of any mistake is that wonderful move of making a decision. This is one of the keys to success. Whether it is a right or wrong decision, you make the move toward thinking positively. When we decide to take a stand for what we have faith in, we are removing the frustration from our minds from indecision. When we make enough wrong decisions in our lives and we have had our fill of hurts, then we learn (but this is the hard way!) we are lacking in one of the basic qualities to succeed.

We must understand the circumstances surrounding our project. We must try again with a new approach. We must realize the mistakes we make are unpleasant at the time we are involved, but mistakes can work toward a positive end. A mistake can teach us never to try that particular design again, or to revamp the design to the point that it will become successful. In other words, reverse your failure and see it as a blessing in disguise.

Keep your thoughts clean and keep them positive; always make sure you do not harm your fellowman. One of the wonderful things about your mind and body is that you can ask for guidance and get it from your inner self. You can demand what seems impossible and it will be there.

You are a great creation; one of the most intricate and precise in existence today. Man hasn't begun to understand all of his complexities. When we take the time to think about the scope of our mind and body, we will realize we are one of the most remarkable phenomena in existence.

We even defy gravity through our blood stream. It flows up as well as down. Our complete system is automatic. We supply the fuel and it is distributed to its proper place to give us the best functioning power. Our complete system is automatic, our breathing is automatic, and we move our muscles automatically and voluntarily to the degree that we need them.

We can apply more or less muscle power automatically or voluntarily for every movement required. This is amazing in itself if you think about it. Let's think a little deeper of the great gifts that we possess and yet so often take for granted.

What would happen if we could not control the amount of power we use in our muscles just in our every day life? Think of the frustration and destruction we could cause. The gentle caress we give something we love would not be so gentle if we didn't control our muscles. Our mind has a built-in radar and guide that tells the muscles of our body what we need and puts it into motion.

Since our mind has this much automation, then by all means, let's develop and help ourselves even more. When we take care of the physical body, we are naturally helping, to some degree, the mind develop. We must relieve the mind from any added burdens such as, over eating, over drinking, or any over indulgence in a destructive form. When we over indulge our habits, we destroy. When we control, we build. We must never split our energy forces within our body as it cuts down on our capabilities to produce. We must, at all times, be in control of our self, and through control, we open the door to our inner sources.

This door automatically opens to our creative forces. We are able to put our full energies into our project, keeping that creative door open for our use at all times. We become more sensitive to the power in the words we think and say, remembering the negativity that is around you in your everyday life, hearing the negativity in speech.

Notice your reaction when you are told of another's turmoil. See the sadness come upon them as they discuss their heartbreaks and troubles. Their shoulders hunch in their own self-pity. Some even look older as the discussion continues. See for them, understand them but remember this is one of the body's responses to negative thinking and talking. Motivate them through your understanding and positive thoughts, to do something about their problem. Don't let yourself become emotionally involved because it will affect your thinking and may cause a delay in your own development.

Words have great power whether they are from you or someone around you. They can affect you in a positive or negative manner. Think of the words "You're fired" and "You're hired". One phrase makes your future secure and one seems to destroy it at that very moment in your life. Use your words wisely and listen very closely. Analyze every situation before you make your move. Accept words as power and realize you are your own material creator.

The success-minded individual admits his shortcomings and makes a special effort to eliminate negative mental and physical traits. Traits such as poor hygiene, bad breath, sloppy appearance, over-talkativeness, poor diction, indecision, over aggression, and the like must be overcome. Strengthen your positive traits, and keep improving yourself in every possible way. Learn to speak with a colorful directness, which paints vivid "word pictures" to the mind of the listener.

Money alone will not ensure happiness. Nor can it provide a complete sense of security. Money does, however, represent a means to the higher standard of living, and therefore is vitally important to you. In order to be happy, place a right valuation on money. In our present economic system, enough money is required to live comfortably and take care of unforeseen emergencies. Be strictly honest with yourself in discovering why you personally desire more money. This insight is essential.

Time is more than money—it is your life! Don't waste it. Get the habit of industry and work to make your time produce financial dividends instead of being of no profit to you. You might "rust" out from not working, but hard work will never hurt you, providing you obtain sufficient rest and diversion. So develop a "work-habit" and study to produce more.

Be interested in people and when you really need advice ask the right people! Successful individuals make use of their personal influence at every opportunity.

Develop your personality so that you can make social and business contacts easily. Be courteous to everyone and make an effort to expand the number of important contacts. It is through knowing the right people that you can advance to a higher level of living.

Learn how to get a "common ground" of mutual interest with every person who is in a position to help you advance. Do not hesitate to ask such favors of those persons, when necessary, and always show appreciation for any such favors granted you.

Be in love with your work, for it is the "vehicle" upon which money comes to you. Learn to make the most efficient use of time. Getting money is always the direct result of effort, either physical or mental, usually both. Remember, every effect has a cause.

The cause which produces money, is a well-planned enterprise, energetically carried out. As long as you show a "benefit" to mankind, and fill a legitimate need, money will flow to you. Do not expend your mental energy thinking merely of "money", but concentrate on legal, common-sense plans and methods of earning money.

The competition these days is keen. Millions of other people also desire the money you are after. These who get money are those whose minds are devoted to earning the money -- not worrying or fearing they won't get it! Center your attention rightly. Worrying about poverty is a sure road to the poorhouse. It tends to bring about the very condition that worrier is constantly picturing to himself.

If your mind is clogged up with poverty worries, clear them out by redirecting your thoughts. There is more money available than you could possibly spend in a lifetime. Start the creative process of your mind working in the direction of that abundance, and you will find money coming into your life as a natural result.

HOW TO INCREASE YOUR INCOME

Think Abundance Not Limitation.   This is the first rule to observe.   Get an "expansion of thought" by becoming more vividly aware of the abundance that is manifested in nature and in the entire universe.   The reason why many people remain poor is because they pay more attention to limitation than to abundance.   Their thought dwells on how little their income is, instead of how large it could be.   This attitude of mind acts as a "circle of limitation" beyond which they would never think of going.

It is a basic truth that you've go to "think big" if you desire to rise in this world, and this applies particularly to increasing your financial income.   You see, the dominant thought pattern in your deeper mind—the subconscious - is built up by the kind of conscious thinking you do from moment to moment.   If you saturate your subconscious mind with ideas of financial abundance, money will be attracted to you much more easily than it ordinarily would.

Therefore you must learn how to put the right kind of ideas before the mental "camera" of your subconscious mind, and let the picture of abundance register there.

Don't apologize for wanting more money. The fact that you desire more money is nothing to be ashamed about. All of us want a greater supply of money, but few people will admit it. False training from early childhood gives thousands of people a misleading notion about money. They misunderstand the instruction that the love of money is the "root of all evil," The truth is, nobody wants money for its own sake.

Dollars in and of them selves are valueless to you except as a medium of exchange. We desire what money represents - the comforts it will provide, the independence it assures, and the self-expression it guarantees us! Desiring what money brings can be a praiseworthy ambition. You are entitled to all you can earn!

Change your "want" to "desire". Change your vocabulary from negative to 100% positive or constructive. Stop using the word "want" and substitute the word "desire." Don't say "I want $1000 dollars" instead say "I desire $1000 dollars!" The word "want" is a poverty word because it also can be taken to mean dire financial need.

The point is, you have to increase the strength of your desire until it is of "white - hot" intensity. Don't be afraid of receiving things. A burning desire is the whole key to getting the better things of life. It impels you to action, and action gets the results. To get what you want, never "wish" for it. Desire it with all your heart. "Wishers" are too "lukewarm" to succeed in much.

Put your silent partner to work for you. The "silent partner" you have is your subconscious mind. This is the deeper, most creative phase of your mind. It will take orders from you. It will work on whatever project you give, and do everything in its power to materialize the financial success you desire. Once given an idea, the subconscious mind carries it out to a conclusion in ways that often seem astonishing.

Since the vast majority of your creative mind power is in your subconscious mind, all you really have to do is impress that part of your mind with your best methods of increasing your income.

Never try to get rich by using your conscious mind only. Get your "silent partner" actively operating in your financial behalf, and you will not have to "break your head" thinking. Learn to let your subconscious do most of the work. That is its' business. Your job is to direct it along the lines of success, ideas, and abundance.

Those who make the most money never try to. They have given a standing "order" to their deeper mind, to create money making ideas. Their mind is a powerful magnet for success, and it matters very little what such persons do for a living. They can make a "go" of just about anything, whether it is selling junk or selling automobiles.

John D. Rockefeller had developed such a wealth consciousness that it was said of him that even if all his wealth were taken away from him, and he was placed in an entirely strange environment, that within two years he would be a rich man again!

Erase all the marks of poverty. The only way to get away from the negative suggestion of poverty in your life is to make a complete "about face." A popular song illustrated this point quite clearly. The lines went "My walk will be different, my talk and my name - nothing about me is going to be the same!" That is the precise way to eliminate the marks of poverty from you. Throw out all your old clothes and invest in a wardrobe that inspires confidence and respect from others.

The psychology of it seems to be this; the business world is not interested in doing business with one who appears to be a "poor risk." If you appear timid or self-effacing, people will instantly see that you are not making a success of your thinking and will naturally assume you can't make a success in money matters either. Change your habit of thinking from negative to positive. Erase the expression of excessive humility from your face. Maintain an expression of optimistic cheerfulness and self-confidence. Get the "lower income bracket" tone out of your voice, and start acting the part of a financially successful individual. Many a person has failed because he tried to be too "saving." Wearing shabby clothing and soiled shirts has cost thousands of persons their chances for promotion and personal advancement in life. Pay more attention to your personal appearance. It will increase your own confidence in yourself, and it will advertise you to the world as an individual who is worth betting on. It is better to miss a meal rather than to skimp on your personal appearance!

Don't hurry - concentrate! The great financial successes never seem rushed for time, Instead of hurrying everywhere and getting nowhere, they concentrate on the one thing they are doing. All their mental power is focused upon the specific task at hand. As soon as the job is done they go on to the next thing and work the same way. The result is, they require less time because their concentration enables them to get the job done. They accomplish in one hour what ordinary men may take three hours to do.

To increase your income, develop an ability to concentrate on one thing at a time.

Forget everything else in the world but what you are doing, and push the thing to a final completion. Practice this principle until you become proficient at getting things done.

Be open-minded. The individual who is not afraid to open his mind to the truth has the whole world helping him. The closed mind repels all help. Success is a manifestation of open mindedness.

After all, we are living in a world where the only permanent thing is change. So we might as well realize that new ideas and improvements are inevitable. Keep your eyes and ears and mind open. High salaries are never paid for mere physical labor but for constructive ideas.

Sell and sell well. You are a salesperson of something, regardless or whether you are selling commodities or your service. To increase your income you have to learn how to market your talents and abilities most effectively and at the highest possible price. If you work for an employer and desire a promotion to a better paying job, sell your boss on the idea that you are worth the higher salary, that you are entirely capable of handling a bigger job.

If you sell a commodity, discover new ways and means of selling it faster and on a broader scale. Concentrate all your energy and thought on a highly specialized commodity or service, rather than on something that is common. By specializing on an item or a service, which provides a high margin of profit, the smartest men and women have found that they can make more money than by spreading their talents over a wider range. It pays to do one thing extremely well, because in serving others best you also serve yourself best.

Use what you have, where you are now. Forming the "Success-Habit" is a matter of doing, as well as thinking. The greatest rewards go to the daring individuals who have an extraordinary amount of "Go-Ahead" in their makeup.

This means you must learn to make decisions quickly, and once you decide on a course of action - go ahead and follow through to a definite conclusion. You may not always be right, but if you get on to the knack of following your inner "hunches" which come from your deeper intuitive self, your successes will soon out number your wrong decisions.

Few succeed where millions fail because most people lack the courage of their own convictions. They fear to make progressive moves when they would do the most good - right now in present time. They are constantly waiting for "something to turn up" instead of improving themselves in every possible way to advance to a higher rung in the financial ladder.

Have a definite plan. This does not mean that you are to attempt to form a "perfect" plan for success, in your conscious mind, and then work that plan exclusively. Nobody ever reached perfection in a single bound. It requires a series of related ideas along a certain line before really big financial success is attained.

Your subconscious mind will furnish all those details as you go along. But it is vitally essential that you give your mind something specific, something important and tangible to work on now. In other words, start the ball rolling in the particular direction you desire to go.

Know how much money you desire to earn per month. Then find out how much you will have to produce per month in order to receive the desired amount of money.

By practicing industry and thrift, and by using the intelligence of both your conscious and subconscious mind, you are bound to make sure progress.

HOW TO OVERCOME THE OBSTACLES TO FINANCIAL SUCCESS

The obstacles to being rich are five:

1.   NEGATIVE THINKING.   Instead of thinking failure, expect success and imagine that success as a definite reality.

2.   THE TROUBLE OF SAVING.   No one ever became rich merely by saving. The fact is, it is extremely difficult to put away money in a savings bank and have it remain there. Too many "absolutely necessary" purposes arise in an individual's life which require the use of that money.

     And even if you do manage to save your money, the interest from it is so small that you have no incentive to save it.

3.   FINANCIAL "LEAKS."   Many big businesses have   gone bankrupt because of financial leaks of which they were not aware. It is one thing to make money, and quite another thing to hold it and manage it.

     Watch the many little seemingly "insignificant" ways in which your money can disappear like water in the noonday's sun.....over-buying, "personal" expenses, smoking, drinking, too high overhead, over hiring of employees, and the like.   Stop those leaks.

4.   LACK OF INCENTIVE TO WORK.   Money is earned through effort in one form or another.

Mental effort pays the highest. If you desire to increase your income, first increase your incentive to earn more. Get some definite purpose for which you desire wealth.

5. THE TROUBLE OF FINDING A PROFITABLE INVESTMENT. Saving money just for the mental discipline of saving, does you no good as far as making a lot of money is concerned, however, constructive saving in the form of investing is another matter entirely. Mere saving is static and unproductive because it ties up your money instead of putting it into active circulation.

The great wealth of this country has been gained by the forces of production on the one hand, and public consumption on the other. The personal fortunes of this country have been made not by saving, but by producing.

The way to wealth is to get into the profit end of industrial production in this country.

This means that you should make a study of profitable stocks and Trust Funds, and other investment options now being offered for investment purposes by various American industries.

Start with a small investment and let it "snowball" for you by letting your investment increase and multiply as the industry expands. If you have a business of your own, plough back the profits into your own business for future gain.

MASTER FORMULA FOR FINANCIAL SUCCESS

In summary review, here is the master formula for what you determine to be financial success:

Step 1 Here is the top secret for advancement! Know thyself. A little self-study reveals things about your personality and your habits, which should be improved for faster progress. Learn to observe how you affect other people.

Are you too shy and timid when with others? Do you monopolize the conversation? Maybe you are too aggressive or blunt in your personal contacts.

The success-minded individual admits his shortcomings and makes a special effort to eliminate all negative traits - such as bad breath, sloppy appearance, over - talkativeness, poor diction, indecision, etc, -- because all such traits irritate other people.

Strengthen your positive traits, and keep improving yourself in every way. Learn to speak with a colorful directness, which points vivid "word pictures" to the mind of the listener.

Be strictly honest with yourself in discovering why you personally desire more money. This insight is essential. Without insight you might make a million dollars, and yet be miserable. Money alone will not insure happiness. Nor can it provide a complete sense of security.

However, it represents a means to the higher level of living, and therefore is vitally important to you. **To be happy place a right valuation on money.** In our present system, you require enough money to live comfortable and take care of unforeseen emergencies that might arise.

Step 2   Use your time profitably.   Time is more than money - it is your life! Don't waste it. Get the habit of industry and work to make your time produce financial dividends instead of being of no profit to you.   You might "rust' out from not working, but hard work will never hurt you, providing you obtain sufficient rest and diversion.   Develop a "work-habit" and study to produce more.

Step 3   Develop Personal Influence. Be interested in people and when you really need advice--ask the right people! Successful individuals make use of their personal influence at every opportunity. Develop your personality so that you can make social and business contacts easily.

Be courteous to everyone and make an effort to expand the number of important contacts.   It is through knowing the right people that you can advance to a higher level of living. Learn how to find a "common ground" of mutual interest with every person who is in a position to help you advance. Do not hesitate to ask favors of those persons, when necessary.   And always show appreciation for any such favors granted you.

Be in love with your work, for it is the "vehicle" upon which money comes to you. Learn to make the most efficient use of time.   Getting money is always the direct result of effort, either physical or mental or both. Remember, every effect has a cause.

The cause, which produces money, is a well-planned enterprise, energetically carried out. As long as you can show a "benefit" to mankind, and fill a legitimate need, money will flow to you. Do not expend your mental energy thinking merely to have "money", but concentrate your mind upon common-sense plans and methods of earning money.

The competition these days is keen. Millions of other people also desire the money you are after. Those who get the money are those whose minds are devoted to earning the money—not worrying for fear they won't get it! Therefore, center your attention rightly. "Worrying" about poverty is a sure road to the poorhouse. It tends to bring about the very condition that the "worrier" is constantly picturing to him.

If your mind is clogged up with poverty worries, clear them out by redirecting your thoughts. There is more money available than you could possibly spend in a lifetime. Start the creative process of your mind working in the direction of that abundance, and keep strengthening your thought pictures of wealth.

Don't struggle or strain in your efforts to get more money. Work with a healthy rhythm. Fill your mind with a clear-cut image of financial abundance—and you will find money coming into your life as a natural result.

REMEMBER

There is a price that we must pay for success. No one has ever accomplished any thing without sacrifice. Don't fool yourself, there is no getting around it. You'll find yourself back at square one.

Life is short and we all have but a moment here on earth. Why waste it in fear, sadness, confusion, and self-denial.

We are going to go through unpleasant events in life, nothing in life is guaranteed, health, wealth, love or life itself. We must change the things we can change and accept the things we can't change.

The human will is one of the strongest forces in existence. We are equipped to handle all of life's emergences. Never allow depression, losses, persons, or public opinion to dampen your will to live life to the fullest. We can fulfill our life's destiny.

There are some individuals who suffer physical pain, daily pain that interrupts their routine, keeps their thinking off balance, and even consumes most or all of their day. This can cause these individuals to be unproductive and to lose prospective on where they are going and how they will accomplish their goals.

Uncertainty is an enemy that causes us to lose hope and vision of our future accomplishments. We must not allow our mind to concentrate on our pain to the point we become ineffective in our daily life.

Most pain can be managed. We must not make excuses for our shortcomings. If you don't help yourself, no one else will. So stand tall and say to yourself I will never give in. Daily living can be a big obstacle but at those times, we must meet it head on with optimism, faith and courage.

It takes just as much effort to give-up, as it does to go on. Why not go on, you just might find that your dreams are just around the next turn.

Fear is the greatest inhibitor of all. More dreams and aspirations have been distorted because of a lie we believed about our self and our abilities. We must over come the oppressive hand of fear; it is our enemy. We fight fear by taking action.

If fear says you cannot climb the mountain, try anyway. If fear says the water is too deep to cross, get a boat or take a plane, but cross anyway. Where there is a will, there is a way! History is filled with stories of those who overcame their fears and succeeded when all odds were against them. You have to love a good fight. So fight the good fight of faith, believe in yourself and never let what other people say keep you from your goal or passion in life. There is no easy or quick way to get there.

You must work hard to achieve your goals in life. The call for help is a wake up call to bring to your attention the need to focus on what is really important in life. Move the obstructions out of your way now!

Your mind is waiting for instructions and direction so it can go to work on your behalf.

Whatever the mind can conceive, it can achieve.

GLOSSARY

a·bun·dance

1.   A great or plentiful amount. 2. Fullness to overflowing. 3. Affluence; wealth.

ac·com·plish·ment

1. The act of accomplishing or the state of being accomplished; completion.   2.   Something completed successfully; an achievement.   3. Social poise and grace.

af·fir·ma·tion

1. The act of affirming or the state of being affirmed; assertion. 2. Something declared to be true; a positive statement or judgment.

com·mit·ment

1. a. The act or an instance of committing. A pledge to do.   b. Something pledged, especially an engagement by contract involving financial obligation.   2.   The state of being bound emotionally or intellectually to a course of action or to another person or persons.

com·pe·ti·tion

1. The act of competing, as for profit or a prize; rivalry. 2. A test of skill or ability; a contest: *a skating competition.* 3. Rivalry between two or more businesses striving for the same customer or market. 4. A competitor: *The competition has cornered the market.*

com·pre·hend

1. To take in the meaning, nature, or importance of; grasp.

con·cen·trate

1. To direct or draw toward a common center; focus. To direct one's thoughts or attention: *We concentrated on the task before us.*

con·fi·dence

1. Trust or faith in a person or thing. A feeling of assurance, especially of self-assurance.

con·scious·ness

n. 1. The state or condition of being conscious. 2. A sense of one's personal or collective identity, especially the complex of attitudes, beliefs, and sensitivities held by or considered characteristic of an individual or a group. Special awareness or sensitivity.

con·trol·ling, con·trols

1. To exercise authoritative or dominating influence over; direct. 2. To hold in restraint; check: *I struggled to control my temper.*

cour·age

n. 1. The state or quality of mind or spirit that enables one to face danger, fear.

cre·a·tive

adj. 1. Having the ability or power to create. One who displays productive originality.

de·mand

1. To ask for urgently. To require as useful, just, proper, or necessary; call for. The act of demanding.

de·sire

1. To wish or long for; want. 2. To express a wish for; request. **--de·sire** *n.* 1. A wish or longing. 2. A request or petition.

dream

n. 1. A series of images, ideas, emotions, and sensations occurring involuntarily in the mind during certain stages of sleep. A condition or achievement that is longed for; an aspiration: *a dream of owning their own business.* One that is exceptionally gratifying, excellent, or beautiful.

dy·nam·ic

adj. **1.a.** Of or relating to energy or to objects in motion. A force, especially political, social, or psychological: *the main dynamic behind the revolution.*

ef·fort

n. **1.** The use of physical or mental energy to do something; exertion. **2.** A difficult exertion of the strength or will: *It was an effort to get up.* **3.** A usually earnest attempt.

en·dur·ance

n. **1.** The act, quality, or power of withstanding hardship or stress: *A marathon tests a runner's endurance.* **2.** The state or fact of persevering: *Through hard work and endurance, we will complete this project.*

en·e·my

1. A hostile power or force. Something destructive or injurious in its effect.

en·er·gy

1. The capacity for work or vigorous activity; vigor; power. 2.a. Exertion of vigor or power: *a project requiring a great deal of time and energy.* b. Vitality and intensity of expression.

en·thu·si·asm

n. 1. Great excitement for or interest in a subject or cause. 2. A source or cause of great excitement or interest.

fail·ure

n. 1. The condition or fact of not achieving the desired end or ends: *the failure of an experiment.* 2. One that fails: *a failure at one's career.* 3. The condition or fact of being insufficient or falling short.

faith

n. 1. Confident belief in the truth, value, or trustworthiness of a person, an idea, or a thing. Loyalty to a person or thing; allegiance.

fear

n. 1.a. A feeling of agitation and anxiety caused by the presence or imminence of danger. b. A state or condition marked by this feeling: *living in fear.* To be afraid or frightened of.

goal

n. 1. The purpose toward which an endeavor is directed.

hab·it

n. 1.a. A recurrent, often unconscious pattern of behavior that is acquired through frequent repetition. b. An established disposition of the mind or character. 2. Customary manner or practice.

hap·py

1. Characterized by good luck; fortunate. 2. Enjoying, showing, or marked by pleasure, satisfaction, or joy.

hon·es·ty

1. The quality or condition of being honest; integrity. 2. Truthfulness; sincerity: *in all honesty.*

in·cen·tive

n. 1. Something, such as the fear of punishment or the expectation of reward, that induces action or motivates effort.

in·ten·si·ty

1. Exceptionally great concentration, power, or force.

lim·i·ta·tion

n. 1. The act of limiting or the state of being limited. 2. A restriction. 3. A shortcoming or defect.

Mind

n. 1. The human consciousness that originates in the brain and is manifested especially in thought, perception, emotion, will, memory, and imagination. 2. The collective conscious and unconscious processes in a sentient organism that direct and influence mental and physical behavior. 3. The principle of intelligence; the spirit of consciousness regarded as an aspect of reality. 4. The faculty of thinking, reasoning, and applying knowledge. Focus of thought; attention.

mon·ey

1. A commodity, such as gold, or an officially issued coin or paper note that is legally established as an exchangeable equivalent of all other commodities, such as goods and services, and is used as a measure of their comparative values on the market. 2. The official currency, coins, and negotiable paper notes issued by a government.

mo·ti·va·tion

n. **1.a.** The act or process of motivating. **b.** The state of being motivated. **2.** Something that motivates; an inducement or incentive.

neg·a·tive

1. Having no positive features: *negative ideas; a negative outlook on life.*

op·por·tu·ni·ty

1. A chance for progress or advancement.

per·sist·ence

n. **1.** The act of persisting. **2.** The state or quality of being persistent; persistency. **3.** Continuance of an effect after the cause is removed: *persistence of vision.*

pos·i·tive

1. Measured or moving forward or in a direction of increase or progress. Very sure; confident: *I'm positive he's right.*

pos·ses·sion

1.a. The act or fact of possessing. **b.** The state of being possessed. **2.** Something owned or possessed. **3.** possessions; wealth or property.

pov·er·ty

n. 1. The state of being poor; lack of the means of providing material needs or comforts. 2. Deficiency in amount.

self-de·feat·ing

adj. 1. Injurious to one's or its own purposes or welfare.

self-es·teem

n. 1. Pride in oneself; self-respect.

shy

1. Easily startled; timid. **2.a.** Drawing back from contact or familiarity with others; retiring or reserved. To draw back, as from fear or caution; recoil.

sin·cer·i·ty

n. 1. The quality or condition of being sincere, genuine, honest.

sub·con·scious

n. 1. The part of the mind below the level of conscious perception.

suc·cess

n. 1. The achievement of something desired, planned, or attempted.

suc·cess·ful

adj. 1. Having a favorable outcome: *a successful heart transplant.* 2. Having obtained something desired or intended. Having achieved wealth.

tim·id

1. Lacking self-confidence; shy. 2. Fearful and hesitant

un·der·stand·ing

n. 1. The quality or condition of one who understands; comprehension. 2. The faculty by which one understands; intelligence. Characterized by or having comprehension, good sense, or discernment.

u·ni·verse

n. 1. All matter and energy, including Earth, the galaxies and all therein, and the contents of intergalactic space, regarded as a whole. 2.a. The earth together with all its inhabitants and created things. b. The human race. 3. The sphere or realm in which something exists or takes place.

vi·su·al·ize

1. To form a mental image of. To make visible. To form a mental image.

wealth

n. 1.a. An abundance of valuable material possessions or resources; riches. b. The state of being rich; affluence.

Will

n. 1.a. The mental faculty by which one deliberately chooses or decides upon a course of action; volition. b. The act of exercising the will.Self-control; self-discipline. A desire, purpose, or determination.

will·pow·er

n. The strength of will to carry out one's decisions, wishes, or plans.

wor·ry

1. To feel uneasy or concerned about something; be troubled. To cause to feel anxious, distressed, or troubled. Persistent mental uneasiness.

www.ingramcontent.com/pod-product-compliance
Lightning Source LLC
Chambersburg PA
CBHW071247170526
45165CB00003B/1268